HOW TO GET UNSTUCK FROM THE ANXIETY MUCK:
A KID'S GUIDE TO BREAKING FREE FROM ANXIETY
AND PUTTING FEARS AND WORRIES IN THEIR PLACE!

LAKE SULLIVAN, PH.D.

All rights reserved. No part of this book may be reproduced or transmitted in any form or by any means, electronic or mechanical, including photocopying, recording, or by any information storage and retrieval system without the written permission of the author, except where permitted by law.

Cover Illustration Copyright LAKE SULLIVAN, PH.D.

Interior Illustrations Copyright LAKE SULLIVAN, PH.D.

CONTENTS

Special Note to Parents 10

What your child will need for this book: 11

Introduction 13

Part I: Understanding Anxiety 17

   Chapter 1: Weathering Our Emotions: Understanding Fear, Worry, and Anxiety 18

      Fear 19

      Worry 22

      Anxiety 24

   Chapter 2: Anxiety: Our Bodyguard for Danger 26

   Chapter 3: Anxiety is Tricky, Sticky, and Icky 30

      Anxiety is tricky: It Thinks it Knows the Future. 32

      Anxiety is sticky: It's hard to ignore it. 34

      Silly paths we get stuck going down: 35

      Anxiety is Icky: It can make you feel bad. 38

   Chapter 4: An Extra Helping of Anxiety: Why Some People Have It 40

      Anxiety: It's Kind of Contagious 42

Part II: Tools for your body 45

   Chapter 5: The Zen Den: Breathe and Relax 46

      Belly Breaths.. 47

      Toes to Head 49

   Chapter 6: Get Grounded: Exercises to Keep You Calm and Collected 52

      Activity: 5-4-3-2-1.. 53

      Activity: Color Hunt 55

      Activity: Animal Spy 55

   Chapter 7: The Big Chill: Navigating Overstimulation and

      Embracing Calm.. 56

      Activity: Blowing Away The Buzz 59

Part III: Tools For Your Mind.. 63

   Chapter 8: Understanding Thinking Traps.................... 64

   Chapter 9: Thinking Trap: Worst-Case Worrying 68

   Chapter 10: Thinking Trap: Fortune-Telling 74

   Chapter 11: The Ultimate Thinking Trap Slayer: Thoughts are Just Thoughts 82

Chapter 12: Dealing with Things We Can't Control 90

    Unhelpful Ways to Deal with Things We Can't Control 91

    Helpful Ways to Deal with Things We Can't Control 92

Chapter 13: Moving from Fear to Action to Growth 96

    Comfort Zone 97

    Fear & Worry Zone 98

    Learning & Growth Zone 98

Conclusion 102

FOR MY CHILDREN.
WHEN THOUGHTS TRICK YOU INTO BEING AFRAID OF LIFE,
REMEMBER FOUR SIMPLE WORDS: THOUGHTS ARE JUST THOUGHTS.

SPECIAL NOTE TO PARENTS

Welcome to *How to Get Unstuck from the Anxiety Muck*, a guide designed to help your child navigate through the challenges of anxiety. This book is based primarily on the principles of cognitive-behavioral therapy (CBT), a proven technique for managing mood disorders like anxiety and depression.

Let's briefly touch upon the foundation of CBT: It's rooted in the understanding that our thoughts profoundly shape our feelings, which, in turn, influence our behaviors. In the case of anxiety, automatic thoughts often skew towards worry and fear, creating a cascade of uncomfortable feelings and potentially leading to avoidance or other anxious behaviors. By learning to identify and challenge these automatic thoughts, we can change our emotional responses and ultimately, actions, giving us more control over anxiety.

This book will help your child understand anxiety and the automatic thoughts associated with it ('Thinking Traps'). It will emphasize the power of self-talk and looking for evidence to confirm or negate fears and worries. We'll also delve into various techniques for managing the physical symptoms (e.g., belly breathing, quickly relaxing muscles, etc.).

One unique and powerful approach you'll notice throughout the book is referring to anxiety as 'it.' This tactic can create a helpful distance between your child and their anxious thoughts. For example, instead of saying, "I am anxious…," your child will learn to perceive it as "Anxiety is trying to make me worry about this situation." This shift in perspective can make it easier to manage anxiety.

The exercises included, such as those in the "Thoughts are Just Thoughts" chapter, are potent tools for people of all ages. By observing thoughts without judgment and understanding that they come and go, it's easier to accept them like "Passengers on the Bus."

It is helpful to remember that anxiety is a natural human experience and has a functional role in our lives, such as keeping us safe or motivating us to act. But seeking professional guidance is essential when it becomes overwhelming or interferes with daily life.

Embarking on this journey may seem daunting, but you are not alone! As a parent myself, I understand the challenges. But rest assured, together, we can equip your child with the skills and understanding to navigate anxiety effectively. With every page turned, we're building emotional resilience your child can draw upon for the rest of their life. Let's begin this important journey together!

SINCERELY,
LAKE SULLIVAN, PH.D.

WHAT YOUR CHILD WILL NEED FOR THIS BOOK:
- Companion journal (see below) OR another journal or diary
- Timer
- Art supplies

How to Get Unstuck from the Anxiety Muck Journal (Optional):

An interactive companion journal that includes all of the journal exercises in this book. This unique journal is kid-friendly and features writing and drawing pages so your child can practice the concepts introduced in this book!

Other books in the *How to Get Unstuck* series:

How to Get Unstuck from the Negative Muck: A Kid's Guide to Getting Rid of Negative Thinking

INTRODUCTION

Sometimes it's hard to stay calm.

This book will help you understand and conquer something we all experience from time to time: anxiety. It'll be your guide to understanding it from all angles. There'll be lots of cool facts and some fun activities too. But the biggest thing you'll get? Tools to help you stop feeling stuck, take back control, and put worry and anxiety where they belong!

Everyone, whether grown-ups or kids, sometimes feels worried or scared.

Maybe you're scared about something bad happening to someone you love or nervous about a big test coming up. Or you might feel jittery about something new or different happening in your life. Sometimes, you might just feel stressed and not even know why.

That's totally normal, and it happens to everybody. The great news is that you don't have to let these feelings take over. You can learn to understand, handle, and even use them to become stronger!

In the next chapters, you'll learn about different types of anxiety and stress and how to manage them. You'll learn to think differently about the thoughts that make you anxious and practice dealing with stuff you can't change. You'll also practice taking action - even when you're scared. The coolest part? Once you know how to get unstuck from the anxiety muck, it will no longer have power over you.

This book is a handy toolkit, but you have the real power. As we go through the book, take your time with each chapter. Do the activities as many times as you want.

Before you know it, you'll feel calmer, stronger, and more sure of yourself!

ARE YOU READY? LET'S GET STARTED!

Pro tip:
Whenever you see **JOURNAL EXERCISE**, get out your journal and do the activity in it. The exercises will skyrocket your progress - so try not to skip them! Have fun!

WHAT YOU'LL NEED FOR THIS BOOK:
- A special journal or diary
- Timer
- Art supplies

Part I:
UNDERSTANDING ANXIETY

Chapter 1:

WEATHERING OUR EMOTIONS: UNDERSTANDING FEAR, WORRY, AND ANXIETY

Just like the sky has many types of weather, we have many different feelings. This chapter focuses on three big ones: Fear, Worry, and Anxiety.

FEAR

Fear is like a sudden clap of thunder or a flash of lightning. Imagine seeing a lion roaming the streets. Scary, right? That's fear. Your heart races and your hands may get sweaty. And thoughts move super fast as you're trying to figure out what to do. It's your body trying to keep you safe.

SIGNS OF FEAR:

- Heart beats faster
- Fast breathing
- Sweaty hands
- Butterfly feeling in the stomach
- Tense muscles
- Hard to swallow
- Feeling cold or tingly
- Want to run away or hide
- Want to cry or scream
- Hard to think clearly or concentrate

When we're afraid, our body reacts in three ways: 'Fight,' 'Flight,' or 'Freeze.' 'Fight' is our body's way of standing up to danger, like if the lion comes closer and there's no way to escape. 'Flight' is our body's signal to get to safety quickly if there's a chance to run away from the lion. 'Freeze' is our body's whisper to stay still and quiet when the lion hasn't spotted us yet.

CHAPTER 1: WEATHERING OUR EMOTIONS

JOURNAL EXERCISE: FEAR

Think of a time when you felt afraid. It could've been anything - during a bad thunderstorm, jumping from a diving board for the first time, sleeping in a new place, or any other time. Try to remember everything about the scene.

What made you afraid?

What did you feel in your body? Mark the ones that were true for you.

___ Heart racing

___ Breathing faster

___ Body shaking

___ Body tingling

___ Sweating

___ Tight throat

___ Tight muscles

___ Knot in stomach

___ Feel cold or tingly

___ Want to run away or hide

___ Want to cry or scream

___ Hard to think straight or concentrate

Anything else?

JOURNAL EXERCISE: BODY MAP OF FEAR

Let's explore and draw where fear feels in your body.

1. THINK ABOUT FEAR:

Take a moment to think about another time you felt afraid. Again, try to remember everything about the scene. Where were you? Was there anyone else with you?

What did you see? Hear? Feel?

2. IMAGINE THE FEELING:

Close your eyes and try to feel the fear again. Where did it show up in your body? Was it in your stomach? Chest? Head?

3. DRAW AND COLOR:

Using the outline of a body on the next page, color where you felt the fear, using different colors for different body parts.

CHAPTER 1: WEATHERING OUR EMOTIONS

WORRY

Worry is like a cloud of 'what if' thoughts swirling above our heads. When we're worried, our thoughts race about things that might happen later. Our brain thinks up many things that could go wrong: "What if making friends in the new class is hard?" "What if school starts and I'm still at home?" "What if others laugh at me?" Suddenly, we're zooming down the Scary Things That Could Happen Highway.

CHAPTER 1: WEATHERING OUR EMOTIONS

JOURNAL EXERCISE: A WORRY STORY

Think of a time when you felt worried. Was it before a test? Big game? Meeting new people?

Now, take a deep breath and try to remember the thoughts going through your head then. What were you worried about? Making a mistake? Achieving a goal? What others might think of you?

Write down your worries using "What if...?" statements.

ANXIETY

Lastly, let's look at anxiety. If fears are lightning bolts and worries are storm clouds, then anxiety is a big thunderstorm. It's a mix of worries and fear.

Fear can make us sweaty or give us butterflies in our stomachs, leading to worry. The more we worry, the worse we feel. This creates an anxiety cycle, like a merry-go-round. Fear feeds worries, and worries feed fear.

Big changes like moving to a new house, starting a new school, or losing someone you love can cause anxiety. But even small things, like getting too much homework or having an argument with someone in your family, can add up and make you anxious too. We'll look at anxiety more closely in the following chapters.

JOURNAL EXERCISE: FEAR VS. WORRY

Anxiety is like a tag team with two wrestlers. Fear and Worry. Fear jumps in the ring first. You feel your heart race, your hands sweat, and your stomach hurts. But just when you think Fear is the only one you have to deal with, Worry jumps in the ring. Worry is sneaky and whispers terrible things that might happen, even if there is no danger. The two wrestlers work together, making it hard to feel safe and calm. That's anxiety.

STEP 1. Draw a wrestler labeled "Fear" on one side of the ring. Draw things like sweaty palms and a racing heart around them to show that fear has brought these things into the ring.

STEP 2. Draw another wrestler labeled "Worry" on the other side of the ring with thought bubbles around them with phrases like "bad things are going to happen" and "what if something goes wrong."

Add anything else you want!

CHAPTER 1: WEATHERING OUR EMOTIONS

Chapter 2:

ANXIETY: OUR BODYGUARD FOR DANGER

Anxiety is like a powerful alarm system in our brain, designed to help protect us from danger. Our ancestors used this alarm to stay safe, and we still use it today. Even though the dangers we face now look different from those our ancient relatives face, the alarm still helps keep us safe!

The two parts of anxiety, fear, and worry, can be helpful. Fear helps us move away from dangerous things, like a car coming down the road. Worry can help us study for tests and prepare for other important things.

However, sometimes our brains will sound an alarm even when there is no real danger. This happens if we worry too much or feel very stressed. It can make our body act like it is in trouble even though it's not. That's why learning how to handle anxiety is important so it doesn't take over your mind and body.

CHAPTER 2: ANXIETY: OUR BODYGUARD FOR DANGER

28

JOURNAL EXERCISE: THANK YOU, ANXIETY!

Too much anxiety can be like a false alarm in our minds and bodies. It's important to listen to our anxiety and learn how to manage it - but also remember why it exists in the first place: it helps keep us safe!

Write a thank you letter to anxiety for keeping you safe. Try using at least three examples from your life where anxiety has helped protect you!

Chapter 3:

ANXIETY IS TRICKY, STICKY, AND ICKY

As we know, anxiety can be really helpful. But sometimes, it acts like a drill sergeant and marches around telling us what to do to stay safe, even when we're perfectly fine. That's okay if we're trying to cross a river with alligators. Thank you, Sergeant Anxiety, for keeping us safe! But sometimes, it just goes too far.

CHAPTER 3: ANXIETY IS TRICKY, STICKY, AND ICKY

ANXIETY IS TRICKY: IT THINKS IT KNOWS THE FUTURE.

Sometimes anxiety can make us worry about impossible things, like zombies taking over the world. We can laugh it off when this happens because we know this will never happen.

But anxiety is a master trickster. And its most powerful trick is making us worry about something that could really happen, even if the chances are very small. For example, we might worry about things like getting hurt or lost or something terrible happening to someone we love. It's much harder to ignore these kinds of worries because we know there's a chance that they could come true. But we'll learn how to fight back against those kinds of worries too.

JOURNAL EXERCISE: ANXIETY'S FUTURE PREDICTIONS

Write about a worry you used to have that anxiety tricked you into believing would happen, but it never did. Remember, it could've be something that had a very small chance of happening, but anxiety made it feel like it was definitely going to happen.

CHAPTER 3: ANXIETY IS TRICKY, STICKY, AND ICKY

ANXIETY IS STICKY: IT'S HARD TO IGNORE IT.

When we worry, it can be hard to stop. It is like snowflakes sticking together to make a snowball. Worries start small but can get bigger and bigger.

For example, you might start worrying about a tiny little pain in your left pinky toe. Sergeant Anxiety says you should start worrying about your whole foot being broken. Then it says you should start worrying about missing your soccer game next week and what your friends will think if you have to wear a cast. Each thought leads to another, and it can be hard to stop worrying once you start.

And, boy oh boy, our brains are very good at finding worries! So good that it can take us down some silly paths!

CHAPTER 3: ANXIETY IS TRICKY, STICKY, AND ICKY

SILLY PATHS WE GET STUCK GOING DOWN:

1. **WORRYING ABOUT NOT HAVING ANYTHING TO WORRY ABOUT.** Sometimes our brains don't believe that everything is okay. So it looks for things to worry about, even if nothing exists.

2. **WORRYING ABOUT WORRYING.** Sometimes we worry about something bad happening. And then we think that worrying about the bad thing will MAKE the bad thing happen. So, we try to not think about it. But then we end up thinking about it more. And then we start worrying about worrying too much. Whew! That's really tiring.

3. **WORRYING ABOUT THINGS THAT ARE COMPLETELY OUT OF OUR CONTROL.** For example, worrying about a meteor crashing into the earth or the weather in three weeks.

When anxiety takes control, our brains can go out looking for things to worry about.

CHAPTER 3: ANXIETY IS TRICKY, STICKY, AND ICKY

JOURNAL EXERCISE: WALKING DOWN WORRY LANE

Choose one of the "silly paths" we sometimes get stuck on when we're worrying. Write about a time when you might have found yourself on this path.

CHAPTER 3: ANXIETY IS TRICKY, STICKY, AND ICKY

JOURNAL EXERCISE: WORRY SNOWBALL

STEP 1: Draw a snowball at the top of your page. Inside this snowball, write a small worry you have, just like the tiny pain in the pinky toe in the example.

STEP 2: Below the first snowball, draw a bigger one. Inside it, write how that small worry could become bigger, like the worry about the whole foot being broken.

STEP 3: Keep drawing bigger snowballs underneath each other. In each one, write how the worry could keep growing. Do this until you've created your own "worry snowball."

STEP 4: Now, check out your worry snowball. Does the biggest worry feel way too big compared to the teeny tiny worry that started it all? Write about how it feels when a small worry starts to grow and grow, like a snowball rolling down a hill.

ANXIETY IS ICKY: IT CAN MAKE YOU FEEL BAD.

Have you ever tried to open a website or app, but it was slow even though the internet was working? This happens when too many things are using the internet at the same time. It's like there isn't enough space for everyone.

Anxiety can be like this too. It takes up all the space and makes it hard for other things to work properly. When this happens, it can cause more problems.

ANXIETY CAN MAKE US:

- Tired and sleepy
- Grumpy and irritable
- Have trouble thinking about anything else
- Have difficulty falling asleep or staying asleep
- Feel tight or tense in our bodies
- Feel bad about ourselves, like we're "crazy," weak, or strange
- Have trouble coming up with solutions to problems or doing things that will help us feel better stomachaches

Sure, let's design a simple exercise to help kids understand how anxiety can take up space and affect different parts of their lives.

JOURNAL EXERCISE: THE BIG BALLOON

STEP 1: Draw a big circle in the middle of your paper. This is your "Anxiety Balloon."

STEP 2: Inside the balloon, write or draw all the things you notice happen when you're feeling anxious. You can use the list above for ideas. Do you get grumpy? Do you have trouble sleeping? Does your stomach hurt?

STEP 3: Now, outside the balloon, draw or write all the things you'd rather be doing or feeling if the "Anxiety Balloon" wasn't taking up so much space. Would you rather be playing with your friends? Reading a book? Feeling happy?

STEP 4: Look at your picture. How does it make you feel to see how anxiety takes up space and what you could be doing instead? Write down your thoughts.

Remember, it's okay to feel anxious sometimes, but it's not fun when anxiety takes up all the space. We can learn ways to make our "Anxiety Balloon" smaller so there's room for more fun and happy things in our lives!

CHAPTER 3: ANXIETY IS TRICKY, STICKY, AND ICKY

Chapter 4:

AN EXTRA HELPING OF ANXIETY: WHY SOME PEOPLE HAVE IT

Some people feel more anxious than others. This is normal because everyone's brain works differently. There are lots of reasons why some people have more anxiety than others.

SOME OF US ARE BORN THIS WAY.

Have you ever known someone with allergies? This means their bodies react differently to things like pollen in the spring. Anxiety is the same. Some people can be more sensitive to feeling anxious. It's just how their brains and bodies work! Nothing is wrong with them.

BAD EXPERIENCES CAN TRIGGER ANXIETY.

When something bad happens, our brains try to help us stay safe. Our brains remember the bad things that have happened before and warn us so we don't get hurt again.

Our brains are very smart and like to learn from other people's experiences too! If someone else has a scary experience, our brain will remember it and try to keep us from having the same thing happen to us.

It's like how cavemen lived. If someone was hurt by an alligator in a lake, everyone else would remember to stay away from that lake!

CHAPTER 4: AN EXTRA HELPING OF ANXIETY

ANXIETY: IT'S KIND OF CONTAGIOUS

Sometimes kids worry because people in their families worry a lot too. It's like what happens when you drop a stone in the water. It creates ripples. Anxiety is like that too. When one person feels anxious, it ripples and can affect others around them.

But remember, it is okay if your family worries more than others. People in the past who worried a lot had better chances of survival. They looked for dangers to keep themselves and their family safe from harm!

If your family is full of worriers, it's okay. Many people have families that worry. Practice the tools you learn with someone in your family and work together to kick the Worrying Habit.

Part II:
TOOLS FOR YOUR BODY

Chapter 5:

THE ZEN DEN: BREATHE AND RELAX

You'll never completely get rid of anxiety. And that's okay. After all, remember why it's helpful. However, when you feel worried or anxious, it can make your heart beat fast and muscles feel tight. In this chapter, you will read about some fun and easy ways to help your body feel more relaxed when you are anxious. Put on some comfy clothes and get ready to learn ways to melt the extra anxiety away!

BELLY BREATHS

Belly breaths are special. Instead of breathing with your chest, take slow deep breaths that fill your belly like a balloon. When you breathe in, your stomach grows bigger like a balloon with air. When you breathe out, the air goes out and your stomach gets smaller. Belly breathing helps relax your body the same way taking a nap or snuggling up with a cozy blanket does.

ACTIVITY: Belly breaths

STEP 1: Find a quiet and comfortable place to sit or lie down. Place one hand on your chest and the other hand on your belly.

STEP 2: Take a deep breath through your nose and make your belly expand as you breathe in.

STEP 3: Hold your breath for a few seconds.

STEP 4: Slowly breathe out through your mouth, letting your belly fall. Imagine you're blowing away a balloon, and it's getting smaller and smaller.

STEP 5: Repeat 10 times. Focus on the feeling of your hands rising and falling.

STEP 6: If your mind starts to wander, gently bring it back to the sensation of breathing in and out.

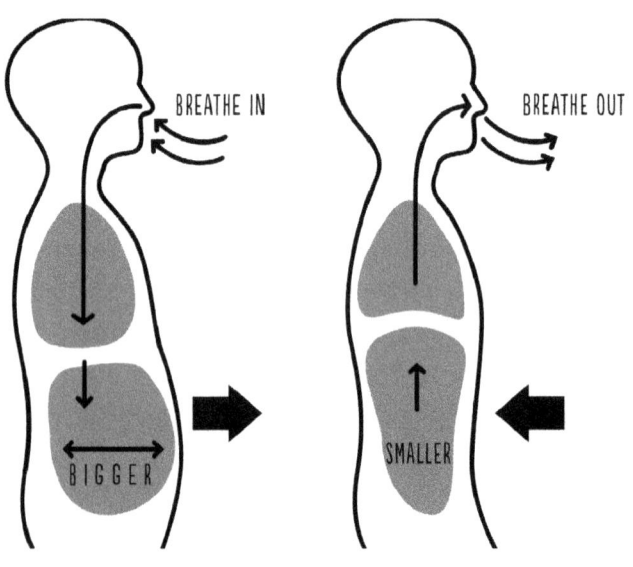

TOES TO HEAD

Toes to Head is a way to make your body feel calm and relaxed very quickly. It's when you try to clench all your muscles tight at the same time. Hold them all tight for several seconds. And then let them all go at the same time. This tells your body to relax and let go of any stress.

ACTIVITY: Head to Toes: Instant Relaxation

To quickly relax your body, follow these steps:

STEP 1: Find a quiet and comfortable place to sit or lie down. Make sure you won't be disturbed for a few minutes.

STEP 2: Take a deep breath in, and as you exhale, tense all of the muscles in your body. Tighten your arms, legs, stomach, squeeze your fists, scrunch up your face and toes -- everything. Hold for 5 seconds.

STEP 3: Now, exhale! Release every muscle at once. Let your arms and legs go limp, unclench your fists, and relax your face.

STEP 4: Notice the feeling that washes over your body. Feel how yourbody is more relaxed.

STEP 5: When you're ready, slowly open your eyes and take a few moments to sit quietly, feeling calm and relaxed.

That's it! You can use this anytime to instantly feel more calm and relaxed.

CHAPTER 5: THE ZEN DEN: BREATHE AND RELAX

ACTIVITY: Imagine It

Imagine It is a game to help you relax. Think of a place you love, like a beach or forest. Make it real in your head and imagine what you would see, hear, feel, smell and taste. This can help make you feel relaxed and happy even if something is bothering you. It's a peaceful trip in your mind!

STEP 1: Find a quiet and comfortable place to sit or lie down. Take a few deep breaths and close your eyes.

STEP 2: Imagine that you are standing in a beautiful, peaceful place like a beach, forest, or garden.

STEP 3: Look around and notice the colors, smells, and sounds in this place.

STEP 4: Walk towards a comfortable spot, like a cozy bench or soft patch of grass.

STEP 5: As you sit or lie down, imagine your body sinking into it, becoming more and more relaxed with each breath.

STEP 6: Stay in this peaceful place for as long as you like, focusing on your breath and enjoying the relaxation it brings.

JOURNAL EXERCISE:

Draw a picture of your imaginary place.

CHAPTER 5: THE ZEN DEN: BREATHE AND RELAX

Chapter 6:

GET GROUNDED:
EXERCISES TO KEEP YOU CALM AND COLLECTED

Feeling anxious can sometimes make it hard to notice what's happening in your body. 'Grounding exercises' are activities that help us feel more connected to our bodies and the real world around us. They're like a 'time-out' for your brain. When we do these exercises, we can focus better, feel calmer, and worry less.

ACTIVITY: 5-4-3-2-1

This exercise will focus on five senses: sight, touch, hearing, smell, and taste.

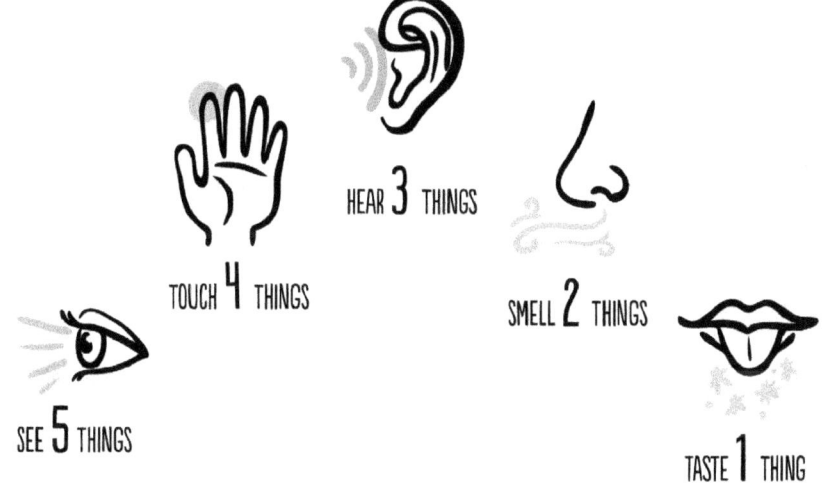

BEFORE BEGINNING, TAKE A DEEP BREATH FOR 5 SECONDS, HOLD IT FOR 5 SECONDS, AND BREATHE OUT FOR 5 SECONDS.

STEP 1: SEE FIVE THINGS

Find five things nearby. Say them out loud, like "I see a computer, a blue pen, a green bench, some clouds, and a painting."

STEP 2: TOUCH FOUR THINGS

Find four things to feel. Say them out loud, like, "I can feel the soft cushion, the warm sun, a cool breeze, and my clothes." Notice things like texture and temperature.

STEP 3: HEAR THREE THINGS

Listen for three things. It could be traffic, birds, or your own stomach rumbling. Say these sounds out loud, like "I hear laughing, my dog barking, and jingling keys."

STEP 4: SMELL TWO THINGS

Find two things to smell. Maybe it's paper, a pencil, grass, or soap. Describe each smell out loud, like "I smell the grass and the woodsy tree."

STEP 5: TASTE ONE THING

Find one thing to taste. Say it out loud, like, "I taste the mint from my toothpaste."

It's okay if some parts are tricky. This exercise helps you learn to focus on what's around you and how you feel.

ACTIVITY: COLOR HUNT

Pick a color, any color! Now look around and see how many things you can find of that color. This helps you focus on the world around you and away from worries.

ACTIVITY: ANIMAL SPY

Think of an animal. Now, look around and try to find things that remind you of that animal. It could be colors that match your animal, shapes that look like it, or even objects that your animal might like. This helps you to focus on something fun in order to bring down anxiety.

CHAPTER 6: GET GROUNDED

Chapter 7:

THE BIG CHILL: NAVIGATING OVERSTIMULATION AND EMBRACING CALM

Imagine you're at a crazy fun birthday party. There's a clown making balloon animals, loud music is playing, kids are running around, there's a mountain of presents, and the room smells like a mix of pizza, popcorn, and birthday cake. Sounds exciting, right? But after a while, you might start to feel kind of funny. Your head might hurt a little, your stomach might feel weird, and you might just want to go home and take a break from all the noise and activity. That feeling is called overstimulation.

Overstimulation is a big word that just means there's too much going on around you, and it's hard for your brain to handle it all at once. It's like trying to listen to five different songs playing at the same time. After a while, it's just too much noise!

So, what does this have to do with anxiety? Well, remember that funny feeling you got at the busy birthday party? When you're overstimulated, your body might feel the same as when you're anxious.

The buzzy, prickly feeling that comes with overstimulation can be like tiny sparks or tingles running through your body. It might feel like your skin is extra sensitive, and you become hyper-aware of every sound, light, or movement around you. It's as if there's too much going on and not enough space in your mind to deal with everything all at once. This overwhelming feeling can make you restless, anxious, and irritable.

Everyone gets overstimulated sometimes, and it's completely normal. What's important is knowing what to do when it happens.

If you start to feel overstimulated, try to find a quiet place to take a break from the noise and the hustle-bustle. You could also try the grounding exercises we learned earlier.

Understanding overstimulation and how it's linked to anxiety can help you navigate through busy days, loud parties, and other times when there's too much going on. It's okay to take a break and rest your brain when you need it.

ACTIVITY: BLOWING AWAY THE BUZZ

To practice calming your system down when you're over-stimulated, try the following:

STEP 1: Stand up straight and plant your feet firmly on the ground.

STEP 2: Take a deep breath through your nose. Imagine you are breathing in a calming, cool breeze. Feel your lungs filling up with fresh air as you inhale.

STEP 3: Let your breath out slowly and imagine the buzzy, prickly feeling leaving your body with the breath. Imagine it as little sparks or tingles floating away into the air, leaving you feeling lighter and more relaxed.

REPEAT 5 TIMES

CHAPTER 7: THE BIG CHILL

JOURNAL EXERCISE: "TOO MANY PEOPLE" STRESS

Think about a time when there were lots and lots of people around, and you needed some quiet time. (Examples: busy family reunion, crowded theme park, busy store after a long day at school).

WHAT HAPPENED?

HOW DID YOU FEEL?

CAN YOU REMEMBER OTHER TIMES?

WHAT DID YOU DO TO MAKE YOURSELF FEEL BETTER?

DID THAT HELP YOU FEEL LESS OVERSTIMULATED?

WHAT CAN YOU DO THE NEXT TIME YOU FEEL "TOO MANY PEOPLE" STRESS?

CHAPTER 7: THE BIG CHILL

Part III:
TOOLS FOR YOUR MIND

Chapter 8:

UNDERSTANDING THINKING TRAPS

Sometimes our brains play tricks on us and make us believe things that aren't really true. These are called "Thinking Traps." It's like looking through one of those funny mirrors that stretch or squash reflections - it's not showing you how you look. Thinking Traps can do the same thing, but with our thoughts.

Thinking Traps are sneaky because they make us anxious without knowing why. They can trick us into thinking we see the future (like thinking we'll get a bad grade) or can read minds (like thinking a friend is upset with us just because they were busy one day).

But we can outsmart these traps. One way is using Positive Self-Talk or saying helpful, encouraging things to ourselves.

Positive Self-Talk is like a cheerleader in our heads. It helps us talk back to tricky thoughts. Instead of saying, "I'm going to do terrible on this test," we could say, "I studied hard, and I will do my best." Positive Self-Talk helps remind us that we are capable and strong.

CHAPTER 8: UNDERSTANDING THINKING TRAPS

Another way is to play detective and look for evidence. This means asking ourselves if there's real proof of what the Thinking Trap is saying. For example, if the trap says, "My friend didn't invite me because they don't like me anymore," we can look for evidence to challenge this. Maybe your friend didn't invite you because they were busy or it was an event with only a few people. Looking for evidence helps our brains see things clearly and avoid getting tricked by these Thinking Traps.

CHAPTER 8: UNDERSTANDING THINKING TRAPS

Chapter 9:

THINKING TRAP: WORST-CASE WORRYING

CHAPTER 9: THINKING TRAP

"Worst-Case Worrying" is when our brains automatically jump to the most terrible thing that could happen. It's like we're playing a movie in our heads, but the film is always a big disaster! Let's say you forgot your homework at home, and your brain immediately says, "Oh no, I'm going to fail the whole grade because of this!" That's a perfect example of "Worst-Case Worrying."

But we can talk back to this thinking trap and look for evidence to challenge it. Here are some examples:

WORST-CASE WORRY "If I don't get invited to the party, it's proof that no one likes me."

TALK-BACK: "Not being invited to one party doesn't mean that people don't like me. I have other friends and other times when I've been included."

EVIDENCE: "Just last week, I played with my friends at the park and had a lot of fun."

WORST-CASE WORRY: "I lost the game, so I must be the worst player ever."

TALK-BACK: "Everyone loses games sometimes. It doesn't mean I'm the worst player."

EVIDENCE: "I remember several games when I played well and scored."

CHAPTER 9: THINKING TRAP

WORST-CASE WORRY: "If I don't ace the test, I'll never get into a good school."

TALK-BACK: "One test doesn't decide my entire future. I can always learn and do better next time."

EVIDENCE: "I've done well on other tests and assignments before."

WORST-CASE WORRY: "My friend didn't text me back right away. They must be mad at me."

TALK-BACK: "There could be many reasons why they didn't respond immediately. They might be busy."

EVIDENCE: "My friend was happy to see me at school yesterday, so they're probably not mad."

WORST-CASE WORRY: "I stuttered during my presentation, and now everyone thinks I'm stupid."

TALK-BACK: "Everyone stutters or stumbles over words sometimes. It doesn't mean I'm stupid."

EVIDENCE: "I knew my topic well and explained it to the class."

WORST-CASE WORRY: "I spilled juice on my shirt. My day is ruined."

TALK-BACK: "A spill is a small thing. It doesn't ruin my whole day. I can clean up and change my shirt."

EVIDENCE: "I've had fun and good days even when things didn't go perfectly."

WORST-CASE WORRY: "I missed the bus, I'm going to be late, and my teacher will be mad at me."

TALK-BACK: "Even if I'm late, it doesn't mean my teacher will be mad. I can explain what happened."

EVIDENCE: "I'm usually on time, and my teacher knows that."

WORST-CASE WORRY: "I got a bad grade. My parents are going to be so disappointed."

TALK-BACK: "One bad grade doesn't define me. I can talk to my parents about it and figure out how to improve."

EVIDENCE: "I've gotten good grades before, and my parents know I usually do my best."

WORST-CASE WORRY: "If I don't go to the sleepover, I'll lose all my friends."

TALK-BACK: "It's okay not to do everything with my friends. True friends will understand."

EVIDENCE: "My friends and I have different interests and are still friends."

WORST-CASE WORRY: "If I ask for help, everyone will think I'm weak."

TALK-BACK: "Asking for help shows I'm brave and willing to learn. Everyone needs help sometimes."

EVIDENCE: "I've asked for help before, and people were kind and supportive."

JOURNAL EXERCISE #1: WORST-CASE WORRYING

Here are five Worst-Case Worries. For each one, talk back to it and find evidence that challenges it.

SITUATION: You accidentally drop your ice cream cone and think your whole day is ruined.

TALK-BACK:

EVIDENCE:

SITUATION: You get a question wrong in class and think everyone will think you're not smart.

TALK-BACK:

EVIDENCE:

SITUATION: Your best friend is moving away, and you think you'll never make another friend again.

TALK-BACK:

EVIDENCE:

SITUATION: You didn't make the basketball team, and you think this means you're terrible at all sports.

TALK-BACK:

EVIDENCE:

SITUATION: Your parents can't come to the school play, and you think they don't care about you.

TALK-BACK:

EVIDENCE:

JOURNAL EXERCISE #2: WORST-CASE WORRYING

For this exercise, think about 3 times when you were "Worst-Case Worrying." It could be about a friend, school, hobby, or anything else. Write it down, then try to challenge it.

SITUATION #1:

WORST-CASE WORRY:

TALK-BACK:

EVIDENCE:

SITUATION #2:

WORST-CASE WORRY:

TALK-BACK:

EVIDENCE:

SITUATION #3:

WORST-CASE WORRY:

TALK-BACK:

EVIDENCE:

Chapter 10:

THINKING TRAP: FORTUNE-TELLING

Do you remember the last time you had to stop watching a movie or TV show in the middle of it? You probably wondered what happened at the end, right? You may have even made up your own ending to the story. We do the same thing with our thoughts. We sometimes act like we know the end of the story when we are only in the middle of it. This is called "Fortune-Telling," and it means trying to guess what will happen in the future.

CHAPTER 10: THINKING TRAP: FORTUNE-TELLING

If we're having a good day, we may make up a happy ending to a situation and expect good things to happen. But if we are stuck in the anxious muck, It's like we have a gloomy crystal ball inside our minds that only shows us the bad stuff. For example, if you have a math test tomorrow, you might think, "I'm going to fail for sure!" That's Fortune-Telling. It's important to remember that just because we believe something will happen doesn't mean it will.

Here are some examples of Fortune-Telling, along with some ways to talk back to these thoughts and look for evidence:

TALKING BACK TO FORTUNE-TELLING THOUGHTS:

FORTUNE-TELLING: "I'm going to fail the spelling test tomorrow."

TALK-BACK: "I've studied and can't predict the future. But I can try my best."

EVIDENCE: "There have been many times I've done well after studying."

FORTUNE-TELLING: "No one will come to my birthday party."

TALK-BACK: "I've invited my friends, who usually come to parties. I can't know for sure, but I can hope for the best."

EVIDENCE: "My friends have come to my other parties."

CHAPTER 10: THINKING TRAP: FORTUNE-TELLING

FORTUNE-TELLING: "I'm never going to get better at soccer."

TALK-BACK: "It takes time to improve at things. I can keep practicing and see progress."

EVIDENCE: "My footwork has improved since I first started playing."

FORTUNE-TELLING: "The teachers will yell at me for not doing my homework."

TALK-BACK: "I can explain why I couldn't do it this time, and they might understand."

EVIDENCE: "There have been times when I've forgotten my homework and they didn't yell."

FORTUNE-TELLING: "My friends won't like me if I don't have the newest video game."

TALK-BACK: "Real friends like me for who I am, not what I have."

EVIDENCE: "My friends and I have fun together even when we're not playing video games."

FORTUNE-TELLING: "I'm going to mess up my lines in the school play."

TALK-BACK: "I've practiced a lot. I'll do my best, and it's okay if I make a mistake."

EVIDENCE: "I've said my lines correctly many times during rehearsals."

FORTUNE-TELLING: "I'm going to drop the ball during the game."

TALK-BACK: "I can't predict what will happen. I'll just do my best, and that's okay."

EVIDENCE: "I've caught the ball plenty of times during practice."

JOURNAL EXERCISE 1: FORTUNE-TELLING

In this exercise, you're going to read about a few situations. After each one, identify the Fortune-Telling thinking trap, come up with a positive self-talk response, and find evidence to challenge it.

SITUATION #1: Jaden sees a giant spider in his room and thinks, "I'm going to have nightmares about spiders forever now."

FORTUNE-TELLING:

TALK-BACK:

EVIDENCE:

SITUATION #2: Erin wasn't invited to Lisa's sleepover and thinks, "Lisa will never invite me to anything again."

FORTUNE-TELLING:

TALK-BACK:

EVIDENCE:

SITUATION #3: Alex got a low score on the math test and thinks, "I'm going to fail math class."

FORTUNE-TELLING:

TALK-BACK:

EVIDENCE:

SITUATION #4: Sebastien forgot the lines during the school play rehearsal and thinks, "I'm going to forget my lines during the actual performance too."

FORTUNE-TELLING:

TALK-BACK:

EVIDENCE:

SITUATION #5: Simone got a question wrong in class and thinks, "Now the teacher will think I'm not smart."

FORTUNE-TELLING:

TALK-BACK:

EVIDENCE:

CHAPTER 10: THINKING TRAP: FORTUNE-TELLING

JOURNAL EXERCISE 2: FORTUNE-TELLING

For this exercise, think about 3 times when you recently had a Fortune-Telling thought. It could be about a friend, school, a hobby, or anything else. Write it down, then try to challenge it.

SITUATION #1
WHAT WAS THE SITUATION?
WHAT WAS YOUR FORTUNE-TELLING THOUGHT?
WHAT POSITIVE SELF-TALK STATEMENT CAN YOU USE TO CHALLENGE THIS THOUGHT?
WHAT EVIDENCE DO YOU HAVE THAT CHALLENGES YOUR FORTUNE-TELLING THOUGHT?

SITUATION #2
WHAT WAS THE SITUATION?
WHAT WAS YOUR FORTUNE-TELLING THOUGHT?
WHAT POSITIVE SELF-TALK STATEMENT CAN YOU USE TO CHALLENGE THIS THOUGHT?
WHAT EVIDENCE DO YOU HAVE THAT CHALLENGES YOUR FORTUNE-TELLING THOUGHT?

SITUATION #3
WHAT WAS THE SITUATION?
WHAT WAS YOUR FORTUNE-TELLING THOUGHT?
WHAT POSITIVE SELF-TALK STATEMENT CAN YOU USE TO CHALLENGE THIS THOUGHT?
WHAT EVIDENCE DO YOU HAVE THAT CHALLENGES YOUR FORTUNE-TELLING THOUGHT?

Chapter 11:

THE ULTIMATE THINKING TRAP SLAYER: THOUGHTS ARE JUST THOUGHTS

You've learned to challenge anxious thoughts and keep moving toward your goals even when they pop up. Now, let's level up to the most powerful skill of all - slaying anxious thoughts by...not doing anything at all. It sounds confusing, I know. But sit tight and put on your seat belt because we're about to go for a ride. And you'll be the driver!

Imagine your brain is like a big, colorful school bus you're driving. Inside this bus are many different characters, like in a cartoon show. Each character is a different thought or feeling that you have.

Some of these characters are really loud and bossy. For example, a character called "Scaredy-Cat" might keep telling you, "Don't try out for the school play, you might forget your lines!" or another one named "Grumpy Gus" might be yelling, "Don't share any of your stuff with your little brother, he'll just break it!"

But here's the cool part: You're the bus driver, not them. Even when a loud character like "I Can't Do Math" starts to yell, you don't have to listen or stop the bus. You can just keep driving, looking at the road ahead to where you want to go.

You might notice some characters being really loud or even acting silly or weird, but you don't have to do what they say. Remember, you're the driver! You get to decide where the bus is going and how fast it's going.

Sometimes, we start doing everything these bossy characters tell us to do. Like if we want to go swimming, but the character "I'm Afraid of Water" tells us not to get in because the water's too cold. You might miss out on all the fun of splashing around with your friends.

CHAPTER 11: THE ULTIMATE THINKING TRAP SLAYER

But here's the secret: those bossy characters are not the drivers. They might say mean things like "You're not smart enough" or "You're going to mess up," but they can't actually steer the bus. Only you can do that.

It's also important to remember that trying to make the characters quiet or kick them off the bus usually doesn't work. It just makes them yell louder or act even sillier. But that's okay because the real problem isn't that the characters are on the bus. It's when we automatically do what they tell us without thinking about it.

For example, Let's say you want to join the soccer team. You love playing soccer, and you're pretty good at it too. But as soon as you think about signing up, characters like "I'm Too Shy" or "I'm Not Good Enough" start yelling things like "Don't do it! You might not be the best!" or "What if you miss the goal?"

But you also have characters like "I Love Soccer" and "I Can Do It" on your bus. Even though they're not as loud, they're still there,  cheering you on with encouraging words like "You love playing soccer, give it a shot!" and "You'll never know if you don't try!" So, as the driver, you can choose to listen to these characters instead and keep driving towards wherever you want to go.

CHAPTER 11: THE ULTIMATE THINKING TRAP SLAYER

JOURNAL EXERCISE: MOVIE THEATER IN YOUR MIND

Another way to think about thoughts is that they are like movies playing in our minds. We can look at them like scenes coming across a movie screen.

STEP 1: SET THE SCENE

Find a quiet, comfortable place to sit. Close your eyes and take a few deep breaths to help your body relax.

STEP 2: CREATE THE MOVIE THEATER

Imagine that you're in a movie theater. The theater is a safe and comfortable space. You're sitting in your favorite seat, the room is just the right temperature, and the chair is so soft and comfy.

STEP 3: THE SCREEN

In front of you is a giant movie screen. This screen is unique – where your thoughts and feelings will appear.

STEP 4: START THE MOVIE

Now, let's start the movie. The movie is made up of your thoughts and feelings. Each scene on the screen is like a different thought or feeling you're having. Maybe you see a scene from school (a thought about a homework assignment) or a scene from the soccer field (feeling excited about the upcoming match).

CHAPTER 11: THE ULTIMATE THINKING TRAP SLAYER

STEP 5: WATCH THE MOVIE

As you watch the movie, remember that you're just the viewer. The scenes on the screen are your thoughts and feelings, but they're not you – you're the person in the audience watching them. Like in a movie theater, you can watch these scenes without getting caught up.

STEP 6: CHANGE SCENES

Notice how the scenes change. Just like in a real movie, no scene lasts forever. A thought about homework might be replaced by a thought about your best friend. An excited feeling might change to a nervous one. This is normal – our thoughts and feelings are constantly changing, just like scenes in a movie.

STEP 7: THE MOVIE KEEPS PLAYING

Remember, the screen remains the same no matter what happens in the movie. It holds all the thoughts and feelings, the happy ones, the sad ones, and everything in between, but it doesn't react to them. It's always just there, holding space. That screen is like you. No matter what thoughts and feelings you experience, you're still you.

STEP 8: WRAPPING UP

When you're ready, take a few more deep breaths, give yourself a gentle stretch, and open your eyes.

ANSWER THE FOLLOWING QUESTIONS:

1. How did it feel to imagine your thoughts and feelings as scenes in a movie?

2. What scenes came up on your movie screen? Describe them.

3. Were there any surprising scenes or unexpected thoughts and feelings?

4. How did your scenes (thoughts and feelings) change during the exercise? Can you describe the transitions?

5. How did it feel to be an observer of your thoughts and feelings, rather than being caught up in them?

6. Was it hard to let a scene (a thought or a feeling) go and let a new one come in? Why or why not?

7. Were there any scenes that you found particularly enjoyable? Were any challenging or uncomfortable?

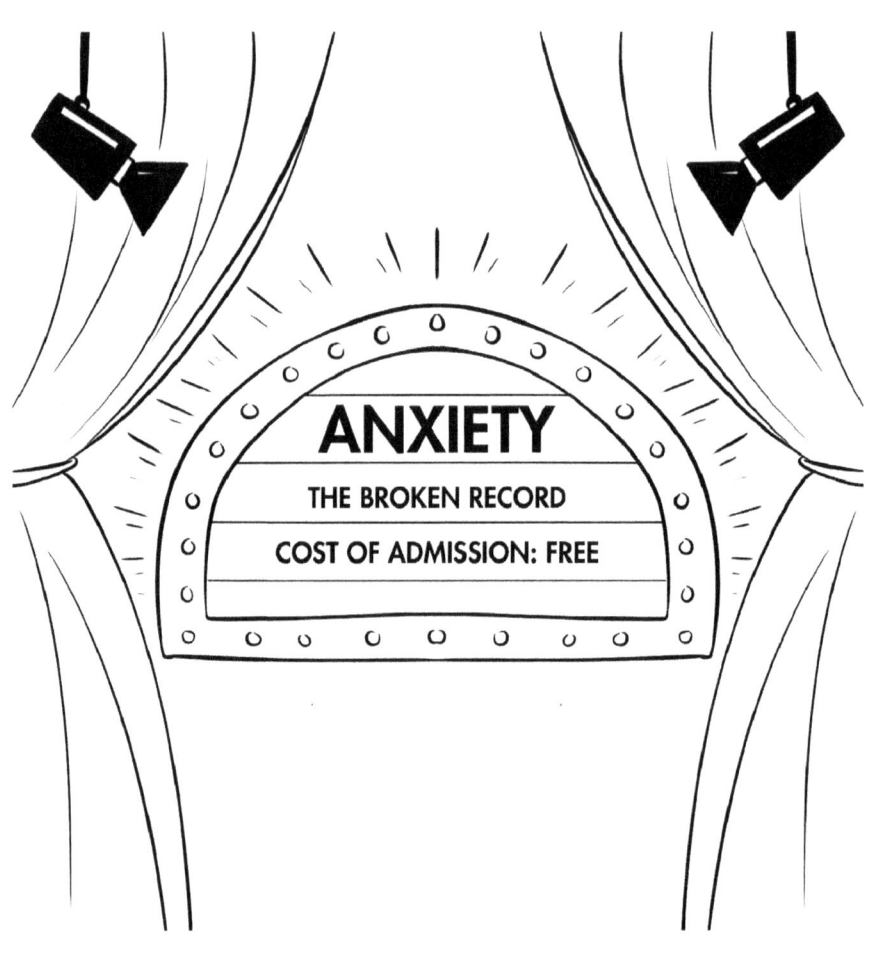

CHAPTER 11: THE ULTIMATE THINKING TRAP SLAYER

8. Did this exercise change the way you think about your thoughts and feelings? If so, how?

9. What was it like to think of yourself as the screen, holding space for all your different thoughts and feelings?

10. Will you use this movie theater exercise again? Why or why not?

11. What was one thought or feeling that seemed to stay longer on the screen? How did you feel about that?

12. What would you name your movie if you had to give it a title? Why did you choose this title?

Remember, there are no wrong answers here. The goal is to become more aware of your thoughts and feelings and understand that they are a part of you, but they don't define you.

Chapter 12:

DEALING WITH THINGS WE CAN'T CONTROL

We all know life is full of surprises. Sometimes, things happen that we can't control. And that's okay! But learning how to deal with these situations in a healthy way is an important skill to have.

When things we can't control happen, people react in different ways. Let's look at some unhelpful and helpful ways people handle situations they can't do anything about.

UNHELPFUL WAYS TO DEAL WITH THINGS WE CAN'T CONTROL

The first one is **CAPTAIN CONTROLLER.** This is when you try to control things too much, even when you can't. For example, you might worry about a big test so much that you can't sleep or eat properly. Trying to control things too much can make you feel bad and doesn't really help the situation. Here are some thoughts you might have:

- I have to get this right no matter what.
- I have to try harder.
- I need to be perfect.
- I have to fix everything.
- I need to be strong at all times.

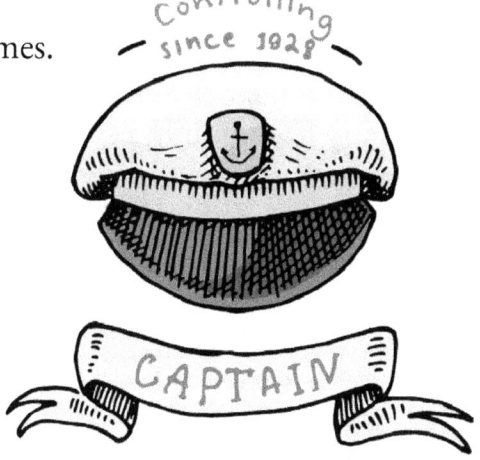

The second one is PITY PARTY. This is when you don't do anything about a tough situation. You might feel helpless or let other people decide what to do. This way of coping can also make you feel bad and doesn't help to solve problems. You might think:

- Trying to change things won't help.
- I can't do anything about it.
- Why do bad things always happen to me?
- I'm unlucky.
- I can't handle this.

HELPFUL WAYS TO DEAL WITH THINGS WE CAN'T CONTROL

Now let's look at helpful ways to deal with things we can't control.

The first one is PEACEFUL ACCEPTANCE. This is when you understand and accept that there are some things you can't change. For example, you can't make it stop raining, but you can take an umbrella and play in the rain. Acceptance is not about giving up. It's about knowing what you can and can't control.

The second one is ACTIVE COPING. This is when you do something to deal with a situation the best way you can. You might not be able to change the problem, but you can change how you think and feel about it. For example, if you're scared about a big test coming up, you can study, ask for help, and remind yourself that it's okay to make mistakes. This way of coping helps you deal with problems and makes you stronger.

In the end, remember that even when we can't control what's happening, we can control how we respond. That's where your power is. And that's how you can feel better, no matter what life throws your way.

CHAPTER 12: DEALING WITH THINGS WE CAN'T CONTROL

JOURNAL EXERCISE: THE PUPPET CREW

In this activity, you'll act out different scenes where characters deal with situations they can't control.

MATERIALS NEEDED:

Puppets or sock puppets (ask for permission to use socks)

STEP 1: Gather the materials. You can use store-bought puppets or make your own from socks and other materials.

STEP 2: Assign each puppet a character that represents the different ways to cope with situations we can't control: Captain Controller, Pity Party, Peaceful Acceptance, and Active Coping.

STEP 3: Decorate each one.

STEP 4: Come up with a story where the puppets face a situation they can't control. Act out the scene, showing how each character would react.

Here are some examples, but feel free to create your own!

- They have planned a picnic, but it starts to rain.

- They have planned a surprise birthday party for a friend, but they discover they got the date wrong and the birthday is actually next week.

- While at the park, one of the puppets loses their watch. They look everywhere but can't find it.

- The puppets were supposed to go on a fun trip to the zoo, but they missed their bus, and the next one isn't until the next day.

- The puppets find a stray dog and want to keep it, but all of their parents say, "No."

STEP 5. After the puppet show, answer the following questions:

1. Which puppet did you like the best? Why?
2. Can you tell me the story you made up for your puppet show?
3. What did each puppet do when they faced a problem? Tell me about it.
4. How did it feel to play the different puppets and show how they reacted to problems?
5. Did any puppet act in a way that surprised you? If so, who and why?
6. Was there a puppet you didn't like or understand as much? Who was it and why?
7. How did it feel to pretend to be the puppets and show their feelings? Did it make you think about how you react when things go wrong?
8. When things don't go your way, how do you usually react? Which puppet acts most like you?
9. If you could make another puppet that shows a different way to deal with problems, who would it be and how would they act?
10. Which puppet do you think handled the problem the best? Why do you think so?
11. If the same problem happened to you, would you react differently now? How?
12. What part of this puppet activity did you enjoy the most? Why?

JOURNAL EXERCISE: THE UNCONTROLLABLE STORY

INSTRUCTIONS:

Write a comic book story about a character who faces a situation they can't control. Have the character try different ways of coping - including both helpful and unhelpful. Try to have at least one character represent Captain Controller, Pity Party, Peaceful Acceptance, and Active Coping. You can choose any of them for your main character, but have the story end with a helpful way of coping.

Let your imagination run wild! Be creative with your story. The situation your character encounters can be anything. Maybe they miss a bus or have to deal with an alien invasion. It's up to you.

If you feel comfortable, share your story with an adult and talk about the reactions of your characters and what they could learn from their experiences.

Chapter 13:

MOVING FROM FEAR TO ACTION TO GROWTH

Everyone tries new things at some point. When we do something for the first time, it's natural to make mistakes or even fail. In this chapter, we'll learn about our comfort zone - a place that feels safe and easy, which makes it hard to leave. But we'll also explore the problems with staying in our comfort zone and missing chances to learn or grow.

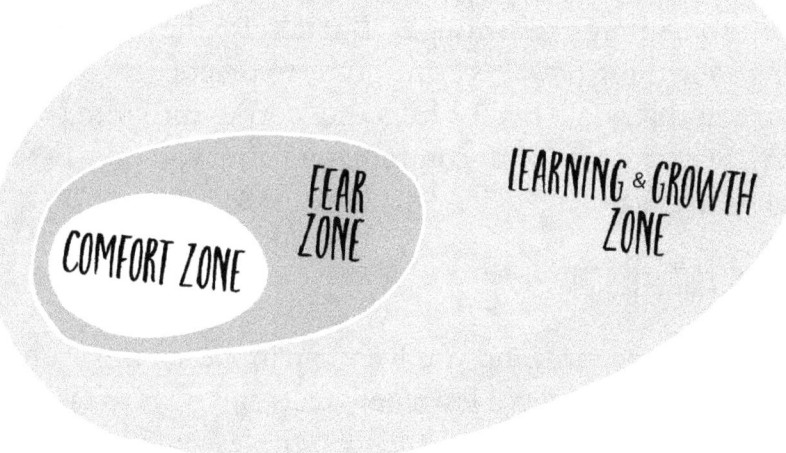

COMFORT ZONE

Look at this comfort zone drawing. The smallest inner circle is our comfort zone. This is where we feel safe and in control. We know what to do here and what will happen. But we don't learn new things in our comfort zone because we only do things we already know how to do.

FEAR & WORRY ZONE

To learn and grow, we must leave our comfort zone and step into the fear zone, the next circle. This is where we might feel nervous or unsure because we're doing things we're not used to. The fear zone is a bit scary - our hearts may start racing, and other signs of fear may appear. Worrying in this zone is also normal (e.g., "What if something goes wrong...") But it's also the first step in learning something new. It's a great time to practice the skills you learn in this book. If your fears and worries turn into panic, it's okay. Step closer to your comfort zone until you calm down enough to try again.

LEARNING & GROWTH ZONE

Keep stepping forward, and you'll end up in the learning zone, the next circle. Here, you'll learn new skills and ways to tackle challenges. The more time you spend in the learning zone, the bigger your comfort zone becomes. You'll start to feel more comfortable doing things that used to be scary. And after being here awhile - you'll begin to shine and feel more confident and stronger. You'll grow!

EXAMPLE:

Imagine you're at school, and your teacher announces a spelling bee. You've never competed in a spelling bee before. Staying in your comfort zone would mean not participating, so you don't have to worry about spelling words wrong in front of your classmates.

If you decide to join the spelling bee, you move into the fear & worry zone. You might be nervous about making mistakes ("What if...") or embarrassed about speaking in front of your classmates because your voice may start shaking, and your hands might get sweaty. But if you push through fears and compete anyway, you'll move into the learning zone.

In the learning & growth zone, you're improving your spelling skills, learning new words, and becoming more comfortable speaking in front of large groups of people. The more spelling bees you participate in, the more comfortable you become. And soon, you're not only comfortable with spelling bees, but you're also more confident. You might even find yourself looking forward to the next one!

If you had stayed in your comfort zone, you would have missed out on all this learning and growth.

JOURNAL EXERCISE: COMFORT ZONE TO GROWTH ZONE

PART 1: PAST CHALLENGES: COMFORT ZONE TO GROWTH

Think of when you needed to leave your comfort zone to grow, but you were scared. In this example, you pushed through it anyway and tried something new. Maybe there was a recent activity at school? Or a new sport?

STEP 1. What was the situation?

STEP 2: Why were you scared or anxious?

STEP 3: How did your body feel when you stepped out of your comfort zone? For example, did you have butterflies in your stomach? Did your heart race?

STEP 4: What were some of your thoughts? Did you have any "what if…" statements? For example, "What if people laugh at me?"

STEP 5: What did you learn, and how did you grow when you pushed through your fear?

PART 2: CURRENT CHALLENGES: COMFORT ZONE TO GROWTH ZONE

Think of something you'd like to try but haven't done so because of fear of stepping out of your comfort zone?

STEP 1. What is the situation?

STEP 2: What scares you about stepping out of your comfort zone?

STEP 3: How does your body feel about leaving your comfort zone? For example, butterflies in the stomach, heart racing, or other signs of fear?

STEP 4: What are some of your thoughts? Do you have any "what if..." statements?

STEP 5: What would you learn, and how would you grow if you pushed through the fear and anxiety?

STEP 6: What tools have you learned from this book that can help you step out of your comfort zone?

STEP 7: What are some things you can do today to move closer to the learning zone? What about tomorrow? What about next week or next month?

STEP 8: If you feel comfortable, share this plan with an adult who can support you in taking steps outside your comfort zone, through the fear zone, and into the learning zone.

CONCLUSION

Sometimes, when we're stuck in the 'anxiety muck,' it can feel challenging to break free. The habit of worrying and feeling afraid can be strong, and it's hard to imagine things any other way. But you now have several powerful tools in your backpack. And just like any new tool, you'll need to practice using it. And you'll probably need to come back to this instruction manual from time to time. That's okay. Even people who have been using these skills for many, many years still benefit from practicing them every day.

TO PUT EVERYTHING YOU'VE LEARNED INTO 3 SIMPLE STEPS:

1. **PAY ATTENTION TO YOUR BODY:** Notice the signs of fear or anxiety. Is your heart racing? Are your palms sweaty? These signs tell you that it's time to take action.

2. **DO THINGS TO CALM AND RELAX YOUR BODY:** Do breathing, mindfulness, and instant relaxation exercises.

3. **THINK DIFFERENTLY ABOUT YOUR THOUGHTS:** Catch Thinking Traps and talk back to them. But, most importantly, remember that thoughts are not real. Thoughts are not facts. Not every thought is important or true. And not every thought is worth thinking about.

You now have the tools to face any challenge, no matter how scary it may seem. So keep practicing, learning, and growing.

REMEMBER, YOU ARE NOT YOUR THOUGHTS.
YOU ARE THE DRIVER OF THE BUS.
YOU ARE THE DIRECTOR OF THE MOVIE IN YOUR MIND.
AND YOU'RE BRAVER AND STRONGER THAN YOUR THOUGHTS MIGHT MAKE YOU THINK.

www.ingramcontent.com/pod-product-compliance
Lightning Source LLC
LaVergne TN
LVHW081354060426
835510LV00013B/1825